Ellen Ochoa

by Rebecca Weber

Ellen Ochoa was an astronaut. She went into space many times.

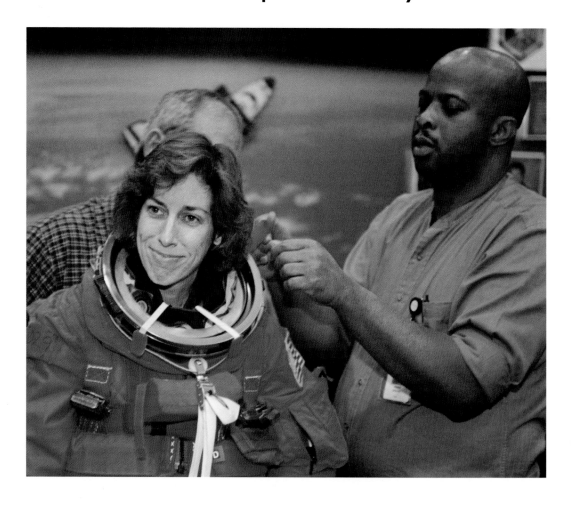

Ellen Ochoa was the first Hispanic American astronaut to go into space.

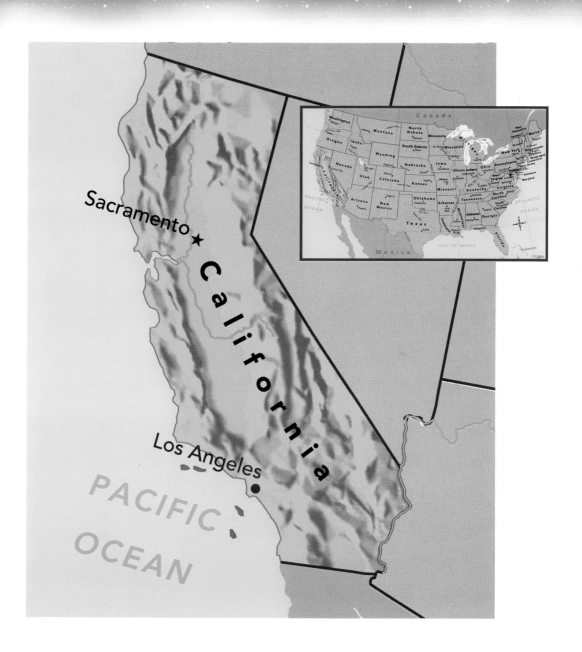

Ellen was born in Los Angeles, California, in 1958.

As a little girl, Ellen liked to do many things. One thing she liked to do was play the flute.

Ellen even played the flute in space!

Ellen also liked math and science. She was good at making things, too.

When Ellen started to work, she made tools for people to use in space.

Ellen worked with other scientists to make different kinds of tools.

Then she worked to become
an astronaut. Astronauts need
to know how to do many things.
They have to use space tools.
They have to talk to people
on Earth. They also have to know
how to eat and sleep in space!

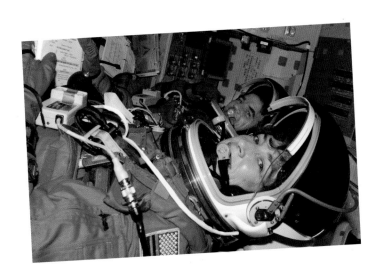

Ellen trained hard to become an astronaut.

Ellen worked hard for three years.
Then she took her first ride
into space.

Ellen took her first space trip in 1993,
on the *Discovery*. Four other astronauts went, too.

On her first trip, Ellen spent 9 days in space. She wanted to find out more about Earth and the sun.

Ellen looks at Earth through the window of her spaceship.

On another trip, Ellen spent 10 days in space. She went to the space station, the astronauts' "home" in space.

Ellen had to go through a tunnel to get into the space station.

One of Ellen's jobs in space was to work the space arm.

Ellen worked the space arm from inside the spaceship.

The space arm is like a big robot. It does work outside the spaceship.

When Ellen was in space, she was always part of a team.

She loved to be with her team, but she missed her family, too.

Ellen holds her son after her return to Earth.

Ellen is not an astronaut anymore. But she still works for the space program. She helps make astronauts' jobs easier and safer.

Ellen is a deputy director of the Johnson Space Center in Texas.